Bene-Dictions

BENE-DICTIONS

poems by Rush Rankin

2002 Winner, Vassar Miller Prize in Poetry
Rosanna Warren, Judge

University of North Texas Press
Denton, Texas

10 9 8 7 6 5 4 3 2 1

Permissions:
University of North Texas Press, P.O. Box 311336, Denton, TX 76203-1336

The paper used in this book meets the minimum requirements of the American National Standard for Permanence of Paper for Printed Library Materials, z39.48.1984. Binding materials have been chosen for durability.

Library of Congress Cataloging-in-Publication Data

Rankin, Rush.
  Bene-dictions : poems / by Rush Rankin.
      p. cm.
"2002 winner, Vassar Miller Prize in Poetry."
  ISBN 1-57441-157-8 (pbk. : alk. paper)
  I. Title: Bene-Dictions. II. Title.

  PS3568.A5715 B46 2003
  811'.6—dc21
                        2002012931

Bene-Dictions is Number Ten in the Vassar Miller Prize in Poetry Series
Cover artwork is by Russell Ferguson
Design by Angela Schmitt

———

ACKNOWLEDGMENTS
Thanks to the editors of the following publications. Some of the poems appeared in earlier versions.
GARGOYLE: *Zeno's Paradox*
PARIS REVIEW: *Why This Poem?*
NEW LETTERS: *Are Academics Funny?*, *Gesundheit,* and *The Utility of Fables*
PLEIADES: *Ghost Among the Branches*
SENECA REVIEW: *Intellectuals at Dinner*
SPUD SONGS : *Tourist Attractions*
5AM: *Form and Content*
KIT-CAT REVIEW: *Reading Palms* and *The Pleasures of Mea Culpas*
RIVER STYX: *What's Repeated*
THE OHIO REVIEW: *To the Former Lover Who Teaches People in England to Think*
THE NEW DELTA REVIEW: *Carnophilia*
NEW MILLENNIUM WRITINGS: *The Largesse of Possibility*

To

Ryan Sparks

who offered me
a more expansive view
of life

and For

Jean Cantrell Rankin and Kate White

CONTENTS

When amorists grow bald, then amours shrink
Into the compass and curriculum
Of introspective exiles, lecturing.

Wallace Stevens, 1923

I

THE TEARS OF T. WILLIAMS AND THOSE OF WILLIAM B.

> In this condition one cannot hear music without weeping.
>
> Nietzsche, 1881

Let's grant even to our own
intellectuals, in their cafés,
a continuing instinct for cafés,
    but not be misled
by table thinking—the chat
that never ends. Words
    too thin and airy
    to register sensation
seldom beat out, as on
a drum, the melodic sign
of meaning, of mourning.

                ●

The lurid thinker's affection
    opens and changes
the structure of thinking
    to include the kindness
of strangers. What you praise
you caress. Picture a person
in love who can still think.
It happens. If I'm wrong,
I've reached the limits
    of my mind, my life,
    and will never know it,
though the world itself
    reflects light.

                ●

    The world's pain
remains unseen, like the paper
    under words. In response
to death, the agents of death,
    those oblivious to death
and suffering—the invisible
suffering of remote victims—
    the naive poet points out
    the hubris of thought,
    its plot, to those killers
    who read poems at night.

•

Certain words suggest indirectly
the invisible movement of planets.
That music of the spheres,
when played, orients the reader
like a compass. The sky swirls
and heaves around him.
To read the effect of rain
on paper, he opens the book
in a storm, as though to find
the world itself in tears.

II

Post Hoc Ergo

I have submitted to a new control;
A power is gone, which nothing can restore;
A deep distress hath humanized my soul.

William Wordsworth, 1807

The Pleasures of Mea Culpas

The collapsed trees along the shore
of his aunt's pond looked contorted
     enough for a Gothic novel.
     A wading egret paused,
shaking his feathers in the shade,
before rising in hurried slow motion
to escape the sudden click of a camera.
It was a calendar scene for the picture
each month of a different bird in flight,
though what he saw, in the dazed blink
of his attention, was the explosive flash
     of just that moment disappearing.
                    •

In nostalgia the past is only endearing,
     like that wise aunt who listened,
even when drinking, to what he thought
was important. Now his writing leaves
     that sticky residue a snail secretes,
those stains left on wrinkled sheets,
as though a person continues to speak
     when dead. That rush of air
of a pilot parachuting from his plane.
                    •

The failure of words gives hope
for something sacred, that tearful
mist of meaning for thick bodies,
that stumbling forward of another
wonderful person, who feels safe,
if nothing in fact can be explained.
     That way he's not the victim
     of his own demeaning clichés
     and Darwin, that rush of air
of a pilot parachuting from his plane.

•

On a porch poised at the edge of a pond
the young man and his aunt sat together
at dusk. The thickening mist of darkness
in the cottage, an eerie haze, they turned
to enter in a daze. Light would show
in dust the fingerprints of their past:
        just walking about on the Persian rugs
        had left the ghostly echo of their lives.
The novel his aunt suggested at dinner
gave that mood an endearing sensibility,
whose enduring presence on the page
        might survive, no matter what.
                    •

        Resembling now a sad turkey
whose limp flesh flaps as he moves,
        he undresses alone in the dark
        or drinks at parties in a trance.
The gentle hostess honors his stupor
        by guiding another drink
        to his hands in the dark.
Even Graham Greene absorbed
        the generous feelings
        he had hurt, had used, to give
his novel the largesse of its mood.
                    •

Tenderness is an accident of character,
        or energy, or just a side effect
of having failed at what you wanted.
        Your excited future appeared
spread out at your feet, like a lover,
over whom you tripped in the dark.
Knowing now that nothing changes
        that finished life, that novel,

you're happy instead at the café
    that flies fish in daily.
Other people spend money to chant
with a Tibetan monk on their yacht.
    As the yacht glides
through an evening mist, the guests,
their skin still glowing with sun,
    are sipping gin on deck.

Are Academics Funny?

In an inner world composed of air,
not water, he might just vanish,
in a trance, in that endless expanse,
the sky itself that illusion of space
the shifting horizon has set in place.

Such a careful, irrelevant professor
putters about like a convalescent
    in his garden, as in a novel
    by Henry James, whose hero,
    at tea, sees all of life in a daze.
In the boorish distance are big cars
that swerve to hit dogs on the curb.
The scraping noise of mangled meat,
    being dragged along, is muffled
by the thick trees which line his street.
        •

Facing the airy academic in class
    are exotic girls who never age,
who linger at a fountain in Florida
on vacation, their golden faces aglow.
It's like some perverse fable. Or test.
Their tattooed flesh draws attention
    to the sullen sigh of their breasts,
    which tired thinkers are expected
to ignore. That's the life of the mind.
        •

That aphrodisiac found in the mutual
    admiration of pupil and teacher
    gives to ideas the daunting feel
of their longings. The whole school
gets excited by the metempsychosis
of inflamed thoughts that change
the disposition of a body. How strange

to see one's heart affected
by how a difficult text is dissected.
Though things fall apart for people
     who breathe and lurch about,
thinkers savor this tender sharing,
     this sweet clinging together,
     while thinking.

     •

Having lived long enough to die
without knowing if he already had,
the prof decided never to undress
again, the fierce joy and sadness
of sex less compelling than a book.
In a naive version of necrophilia
an aroused maiden sees pleasure
in the severe aesthetic of a skeleton,
whose bones might come to life
in her flesh. A person longing
for the unexpected thus dreams
of finding a rare antique in the attic.

     •

Why monitor the dazed glances
of those eager lovers in the dark
or even that couple who parked
above the town? Aren't misty
lights the echo of distant stars?
A crooning voice on the radio
shapes a thought to that flesh
changing form under clothes.
     The bureaucratic standard
for disrobing remains merely
a matter of when or whether,
of dishabille and décolletage,
and the emperor just seeing
     what's never there.

●

The sitting academic softens
in his chair. Too busy living
different lives in different books
    he fails to confront
    what never changes,
    the force of falling trees,
and people. There are even
    bitter people, sipping beer
in their truck, who'd throw him
through a bar's gigantic mirror.
    "Well," his wife said, in bed
    one evening, "a little bit
    of you goes a long way."
●

If he doesn't recall his addled mother,
who talks to her dead husband all day,
or his crazy brother two Marines
always follow in a jeep, or think
of his dead sister, whose frail body
a surgeon dismantled, one chunk
at a time, or his drunk father who died
too young to stay silent when dead,
his cry a long, empty, raging lament—
    well, then, he turns another page
and looks up, in class, at both the dull
and the shining, eager, expectant faces.
●

At times, his mind goes blank in class,
or at the bank, a gap through which
one day he'll vanish. He knows then
that death provides that theory
    whose evidence disappears
    each time a person dies.
In the indecent joy of his thinking
the intellectual lectures those dead
thinkers so brilliant they applaud

even without hands this brilliant
    version of their thought.
               •

For an aging professor the expansion
    of mind exceeds the dissolution
of body, he thinks, though he's told
    to go sit nobly in the snow
    like a statue, while the tribe
takes off again. On the return trek
the following spring, they discover
    his melted carcass, still bent,
    of course, around his final book,
looking pretty much the same as usual.
He must have fallen asleep while reading,
they say, *and so never heard us leaving.*

The Utility of Fables

Maniacally rowing a metal boat
across the lake in a storm, seated
    backwards, the poet pictured
    the synaptic leap of lightning
through his mind. In his wife's
large eyes focused on the future
at his back, he saw the storm
    approaching from behind.
    Later, at their island cottage,
to finish the fable, the marriage,
    an expiring bulb
    flashed into darkness.

                •

Now a harried bachelor, the poet
read while he ate, as though food
were a minor part of the story,
and other people a mistake. Until.

                •

Kelly Spires' new job selling books
(for a group of university presses)
took her out of the city for weeks.
She liked the honesty of greed
    and credit cards and people
    nodding when you speak.
Some people thought her figure,
    her presence, gave the world
    its focus, and thus guaranteed
the success of books she touched.
    Her own intellectual projects
she dropped, as though freeing herself
    from something shameful
    and a poet. His usual trance
    was now engulfed by another,
by her, as when a person sleeping

also dreams. Suspicious
of romantic claims, or so
she said, Kelly turned over
when told. Stretching out slowly,
as in a trance, oblivious
to the normal clamor
of events, she detected
in the distance a scream,
whose vibrations she absorbed.

•

Philosophic time reduces all groans
to tenderness, said Henry James.

•

One night, when naked, the poet held
Kelly naked in his arms as she slept.
His skin, exposed to the pressure
of her body for hours, he hoped
would retain that imprint
longer than a thought. Careful not
to wake her, reaching down, he parted
her legs, which lazily adjusted
to his hand. His probing finger
absorbed her mute response
as she slept, her body swelling
into an unvoiced sigh, as the tremor
of those soft contractions, so endearing
to him, then deepened her sleep.

•

Napoleon, said Kelly, paused
in battle to send his lover a note:
"Don't bathe; see you in three days."
The two lovers, sprawled on the bed,
and glistening, as though posing
for an Impressionist painting,
then gently examined each other
by tilting the lamp. The pigment

applied to the scene, in their eyes
    a reflection of themselves,
eventually would dry. If their
full portraits escaped the frame
    and moved on, they'd only
be ghosts, that reflection seen
through in each window passed.

                    •

The noisy, drunken party at the house
    Kelly entered with her other lover
the next night echoed out to the street.
Like the paralyzed body in a morgue,
the poet wiggled one finger, as a sign,
but Kelly just stared, as she passed,
    as though peering out of a dream.
Branches shifted stiffly in the icy wind.
Standing still for a moment, a silhouette,
the poet expected a different life to begin.

                    •

    Later that night and drunk
in a spooky place among elusive
    friends when leaving a bar
    to search among shadows
for his forgotten car, he sensed
that some stranger had stolen
his life. Yet the time that Kelly
asked about death, as threat
and stimulation, and the poet
    did nothing, just grinned
like her, it was she who left.

                    •

Death forms a vague mist in the moist tissue
    of the brain. If a surgeon lances
    the brain, it feels nothing, nothing.
    That strange fact confuses people
    who think, while a severe angel

remains poised against the sky.
The poet's sister in the hospital now,
*   her face bloated and twisted*
by disease into a swollen mask,
*   impaled now at the center*
of some fatal pain, she jerked away
when touched. And each heart,
*   clutching, squeezes out*
*   its redundant blood.*

●

As the poet sat at the picture window
of the Palestinian café, safely watching
life in the street, a screaming ambulance
flashed past toward some frantic drama
in the distance, where people gathered.
The chef's chicken entrée was famous
among arty people and intellectuals
who dressed, like stylish mourners,
in black. Though lousy restaurants
formed the city's norm and culture,
its mute ideal, this old-world café
valued conversation with coffee
and easy laughter and the hint
and hope of ancient struggles.
Serious, well-mannered waiters
looked sad when they smiled,
    as though attuned to fate.
In a panoramic photo of Jerusalem
covering the back wall, everybody
had paused, as though to think.
The weariness and fever of living,
the groundswell of muffled groans,
was silent, like paper, like time.

●

Philosophic time reduces all groans
to tenderness, said Henry James.

•

The poet scribbled his own silent notes on paper.
If you followed the ink back into the pen,
the pen into his hand, to find his arm,
his body, from which the world spread
like rays, in every direction, just as Ptolemy said—
then the three dimensions of that moment
showed their form, but vaguely, like a light
turned on in a lighted room.

•

At the café, the poet heard himself
invited to Grace Stern's table
to hear a sad story about a friend.
Grace was another lapsed intellectual,
now a call girl, whom the poet
had heard about from a mutual
friend, who was himself, like Grace,
a savvy veteran of the demimonde.
Her shapely body tightened
by surgery, only her mouth moved
when she cried. Though weird
and scary, like her tears
in public, a call girl's shady life
intrigued a poet so naive still
about what happens at night.
In that tricky labyrinth, after all,
a wild bull paws the ground.
Grace's grinning lover at parties
often posed an unnerving question
about sex that felt too blatant
to be answered without saying
too much. The pressure of this odd
vulgarity, like a naked priest
with a whip, distorted the real force
of both an easy affection and lust.

In that tricky labyrinth, after all,
a wild bull paws the ground.
A simple twist or fact, or disarming
attitude in a mystery, that cat asleep
on a coffin, deflects each thought
from what's really strange.

To the Former Lover Who
Teaches People in England to Think

A brilliant, nude woman
with sweet intentions, rather than just
interrupting our sadness, he said, provides
all the mystery there is.

Molly B. Books provides a coffee bar,
old stuffed chairs, and used books.
There's even talk of Michelangelo
among the regulars who come and go.
The turned pages of books neatly layer
increments of time. The shiny covers
of new books now appear too harsh
and bright, too slick. Old books
    have the consoling feel
of some secret, endearing life.

        •

    Not making what he can't make
into poems, he recommends sympathy,
instead, for the humanism of failure.
    Being helpless inspires affection,
and regret, and gives an endearing
distance to pain, like the last photo
of a person still alive. For that picture
    he pauses, then turns away,
the surface of his face left behind.

        •

Her nervous body, so quick, so efficient,
her thrilling remorse and good will
when considering sex, he craved less
than her mind. What she urged in bed,
in a stutter of affection, she provoked,
    like a stock broker who is trusted.
Even in public she touched her lover
all the time, as though he needed

her conviction, her courage
when she punched a rude guy in the bar.
Somehow a persistent hope, a longing
for babies and publication, has survived
    her pampered life at Cambridge.
Clever, but jaded thinking at high table,
among self-obsessed, successful men
still shifts towards her, to test ideas,
their range and results, no matter
the jokes mumbled when she passes.

●

Beautiful, but too easy to please,
she feared her lover was bored
after sex, after the shower, after
toweling off, when the mystery
of romance, wiped away, revealed
    only that obvious body.

●

A brilliant, nude woman
with sweet intentions, rather than just
interrupting our sadness, he said, provides
    all the mystery there is.

●

Writers specialize in sitting down,
    but if he could live another life,
    he'd open her door, like a book.
Her apartment in a former convent
liberated by Henry VIII, who liked sex
more than God, has a thick door
    that's heavy, but reassuring,
    like a big history book.
The latest sonar equipment detects
those voices still immersed in matter.
The subtle shapes of sound waves
    encode in a porous substance
a portrait of that speaking person.

Even in bed they'd only chat,
with no fixed subject, no results,
just like clever thinkers in France.
•

People not obsessed with books he envies
when needing money more than hope
and meaning. If a vacation, like a scene
in relief, exposes a shapeless life, still,
the thinking soldier savors his cigarette.
Nothing moves us less than a person
    deeply moved by his own drama.
Not really depressed, but a Buddhist
happy to have accomplished Nothing,
he still sees what birth control begets.
Only a person alert to Darwin feels
the force of life, those words, those
arms extending to him a real baby.
•

Beyond the quantum force
    of implausible attractions
across the vast pathos of space,
as in the mysticism of marriage,
mechanical experiments now show
    that tiny, steel balls bouncing
    on a vibrating tray actually
bounce into oval and funnel forms.
Implicit formal properties in matter,
    you see, our own actions free,
just as Aristotle said. That person
in marble Michelangelo touched
he exposed, though it embarrassed
the Pope, whose body throbbed
underneath his robes. His words,
he hoped, he prayed, echoed a life
    of their own, like arms
extending to him a real baby.

Greta Garbo in Dark Glasses

That distant howling you can't hear,
but might, the possibility inherent
    in an empty, vibrating space,
is really just a fact of life, a secret
form of noise, as when a stranger
    is screaming under water.

•

Shy mosquitoes on the porch at dusk
probe for a patch of exposed skin,
like awkward, impatient doctors.
    For the couple living together
long enough, the failure to honor
    the other's deepest longing
leaves them both stranded in a movie
    that's over, the dazed crowd
streaming out into the evening.
A life falls apart in slow motion.
You might watch the silhouettes
of birds settle in the trees at dusk.

•

Drained by the fever of messy sex
Augustine ignored both God and Mama
until finding in a mea culpa the logic
    of a guilty pleasure. To show God
while preaching, he pointed at the sky,
    which was large enough to absorb
even the loudest scream in the world.

•

Though too pleased by solitude,
whether napping on the porch
or reading Augustine, whether
dazed by love, or even depressed,
like Greta Garbo in dark glasses,
you still think your lover deserves

an ideal devotion. So you picture
in the future a lament, a longing,
for just this troubled past.

Intellectuals at Dinner

During dinner we complained
like stunned tourists at the seashore
after a storm. *In surgery on the brain*
    the brain itself doesn't feel pain,
I said, in a kind of vague parable.
Though we praised eager people
    who talk without touching
    each other under the table,
we still denied the political take
    on any subject we ignored.
      •

After sipping wine, one friend
    described the burglar
she saw in her room one night,
as though she were dreaming.
He left her shaking, the pressure
of a weapon against soft flesh.
Then, accepting herself better,
affirming her own compulsions,
her new focus, she confessed
    she too had bought a gun.
      •

We did agree that intellectuals
suffer, no matter how effete
    we sound to other people.
    When we toasted friendship
our pretense was more important
than a useless truth. There was
talk of death, but no mention
of that child who killed himself.
      •

We'd seen a person in a movie
    survive his death
inside the actor's life, his fame,

whose shiny meaning itself
    was like a movie. Since
what we said was incomplete
we couldn't scream or embrace
or sob the way excited actors do.
    And our flesh, like lava,
was spreading all around us.

•

*   The children who had not*
*   killed themselves stopped*
by several times that evening
*   on their way to another*
secret meeting. They smiled
when we spoke to encourage
our romantic faith in words.
*   Through the open door*
we saw the darkness
glowing, and the dense trees,
among which they'd spend
the night. And we hoped
*   they'd be amazed only*
*   by what was harmless.*

III

SEISMOGRAPHIA

Was not writing poetry a secret transaction,
a voice answering a voice?

Virginia Woolf, 1928

Ghost among the Branches

He could not cry out, I am a poet!
James Salter, on Lorca

So many poets are delicate
and talk to angels, in the manner
of Rilke, or spray a fine mist in the air,
to simulate a gentle mood at dusk.
•

Only a great poet under pressure
sees a dead angel in an orange tree
      behind his house, as Lorca did,
and whispers words that are like dust
      on an orange. The actual fingers
      of a poet leave their trace in dust.
Perhaps the wind lifts a white sheet
      into the air which settles in a tree
near an eager poet, who then looks up
at an odd ghost among the branches.
•

The dazed poet wants the best deal
      for a mortgage, yet would seal
in rhyme the awkward longings
of his heart. That inclusive version
of social shaping allows the soul
the sweet vulgarity of people
      touching.
•

A movie shows each window
of a train reflecting what flashes past
at a set number of frames per second,
      in that dizzy glimpse a history
too grand for any guide to picture.
      In Greece, in front of tourists

who idle past, naked people in stone
endure the spell of their greatness.

•

As the only person in America now free
and outrageous enough to be honest
and discreet at the same time, who has
an eloquent affection for the improper
groping about of desire, while alert
to the lurid suffering of other people—
only her, that woman from Louisiana
who curses, who smiles, will perfect
    a candid version of the baroque.
With her droll demeanor, her jokes
(and bourbon) offer consolation at dusk.

•

Even the Loud Poet speaks in a hush,
like a pleading lover on the phone,
in spite of himself, his resolution.
He too talks to God like any lush
who can't hear himself speaking.
    At a New Age party in the home
of a paraplegic, or upper class maven,
or a tribe whose totem is the raven,
    only other people have ears.
Only they know what he can't hear.

•

    Picture the orange Lorca peeled
and ate, the juice dripping on his pants,
one day, one year, before the Fascists
    took him to a vacant, silent field,
    where he screamed once, forever.
    A door opened in the darkness
too soon, too soon, that film exposed
    to the blinding flash of his life.

Carnophilia

At ground zero, we see just pieces
    of shredded paper, that scream
of fragments, falling from the sky.
    Beliefs only change when already
they have, not with talk, but the pressure
of life. Sure, maybe later, as you drink
at the bar, a troubling retort hits home,
like an invisible ray from outer space.

            •

For befuddled people who can't
    affirm God, nor the ecology
of decay, nothing justifies death.
Though Buddhists say everything
is Nothing, in a sentence so large
it doesn't exist, they still wave
at the Buddha, who is very fat.
Ghosts, of course, are just people
in sheets playing Trick or Treat.

            •

Amoebic flesh, that embrace,
    that sponge, records
    the felt echo of events,
as when lights glitter like hope.
    If an idea holds water
in a glass, we say: gurgle, gurgle.
We avoid then those vague terms
    that lack the limpid force
    of whiskey in the evening.

            •

It's not what clothes conceal or reveal
that's mysterious, but the naked body
    itself, when animated by desire,
with just a few candles here and there,
and a glass of wine: gurgle, gurgle.

Though we lurch about in the dark
      like deaf and dumb wrestlers,
though the only true Darwinists
still swinging among the vines
are Catholics, though we suffer
      the "little death," so called,
and its brief lament, still, we praise
      what an excited body can do.

                    ●

I propose no political frame,
or boundary, no elevated or debased
perspective, I think not of power
that warps even what it disclaims
and represses—or all the dangers
of praise, in whose tension even
a redemptive moment must strain—
no, here I picture particular people
in whom a note of grace appears
      and a deft, endearing touch.

                    ●

One night at a conference a certain
famous, indeterminate thinker
      scratching at a hotel door
begged a very beautiful thinker
(being real herself, like a thought)
      to let him in. A true story,
or so I'm told. When French
words encountered the American
      body of thought at Oxford
no paradox helped. The closed
      door remained a door
      and closed. There was
      a whimpering in the hall.

•

A woman practicing sign language
   in her car discovered a man
had followed her home. The sense
she made he took from the air.
   If not just his projection
   or her paranoia, or rape,
that's art. In art, a begging man
   in a hotel shuffles about
on his knees. In art, a woman
in her car waves her hand
like a scream. A greeting.
   Like a benediction.

A Touch-and-Go Process

If an idea immersed in flesh
speaks its version of the body,
you see a person breathing.
    The specific details
then shape each summary
of the world, like a scream
in the middle of the night.
                    •

People free of contradiction
I admire, but my own oblique
thoughts stumble about. If
I walk into a cloud of perfume
on the sidewalk, I wonder
what life I missed. I resolve
an idea by living through it—
a real touch-and-go process,
like an unexpected divorce.
                    •
To follow logic, we strain,
like a drunk when tested,
    to walk a straight line.
The shape of each moment
after the fact then appears
incomplete. Of course,
    most of life is obvious,
thus implicit, thus ignored,
    thus really a secret.
What the delicate mystics
    call an "inner light,"
Matisse found at the beach
    at dawn, the quiet sea
    glowing, like an eye.

•

If you admire some famous
version of an invisible God,
    or the latest obtuse
French idea, and thus claim
you can't see, your vision
    a blur, like a painting
    left out in the rain,
then you aren't Van Gogh,
who records the gleaming
sadness of trees, of stars,
his bright colors a prayer.

Gesundheit

One serious friend who swims
    a lot attributes to water
the consolation of massage.
The pressure of deft hands.
Content with sublimation
    she visits monks
who are smart, but quiet,
in thick-walled rooms,
    the vaulted chapel,
each murmur an echo
that fills cosmic space.
          •

Different folks need different
fables, the way a swimmer,
in the history of evolution,
    likes fish, as an ideal,
as an entrée. Freud said
sick people who disagree
with him demonstrate
    their sickness
    by disagreeing.
So let's trace out an idea,
not in the dots, the dust,
    of the mind, but later,
when the body spreads
around it, like an echo.
          •

Because a drug addict
    with a gun screamed
at me like a tree splitting
    apart, I now read a lot.
And when you die, gasping
for breath, yes, your body
tightening, yes, what book
    drops from your hand?

●

A drunken father on a farm
stuffed wild, twisting cats
    screeching into a sack,
which he hung from a limb,
then aimed his rifle and fired
    and fired again
at those frantic screams
in the sack. That echoing crack
    of the rifle ripped open
    the forest. And the boy
watched, in shock, as each shot
    passed through the cats,
the tree: and just kept going.

●

Needing a distraction,
a focus, as compelling
as strip poker, needing
    the grace of thin,
naked people dancing
    on the lawn, we beg
    for help. What style
of confession, like a bump
and grind in formal attire,
grants that vulgar person
    his delicate life?

●

His lover slipped up behind
the intellectual at his desk,
to put her hands around
    his eyes, and ask,
"Guess who?" Shutting
his dictionary, unfolding
    her body, he prayed
to God for help. Oh God,
    he said. Oh God.

●

At his subway stop,
when he climbs to the street,
when the sun sweeps over
his face, does he sneeze?
What might he remember
of the beggar musicians,
the weight of the earth
compressing their sounds,
   the dense echoes,
   and sadness?

Reading Palms

Poets are irresponsible people who
enjoy the privilege of poetic license.
Freud, 1933

The poet at the bookstore
considers the escalator
a *deus ex machina* for tired poets.
In the books he reads he fights
through the messy details
of his own life, as though clever
strangers had collected
the secrets of his past:
those sad lovers
framed in the storm
by a sudden flash of light
the darkness that follows
obliterates. His hippie wife
hinted, for example,
that her tenderness of heart,
if nothing else, explained
her affair with a saint.

•

Escalators don't show the full motion
of the mind, but the working notion
of mechanical steps, which float
people, like statues, to the next floor.

•

The poet's version of group sharing,
that rhetorical "we" of the preacher
caught sleeping with the choir,
avoids the queasy holding of hands.
That wary poet then reading palms
wears gloves. Even after
insulting the Pope, whose protocol

was power, Michael Angelo offered
  just one limp hand to God.
                •

In the canonical force of great words
  the center holds no matter what
happens to birds: the widening spiral
of their flight leaves the empty page
  of the sky. Picture a giant
perplexed when touching himself.
No matter their weight, their longings
  fading like a scream, those sweet
but tiny lovers, and his large, blaring
  obsessions, all fell through space
  at the same speed, as in a dream.
                •

Escalators don't show the full motion
of the mind, but the working notion
  of mechanical steps, which float
people, like statues, to the next floor.
                •

  The vicarious life requires a book
or bed, the body itself a kind of Braille
for that naive lover who reaches out.
  Pert breasts displace the medium
of their passage, like a shapely prow
at sea. Are rumors of a sexual thrill
  the result of the shiny silver stud
  in her tongue? Though the poet
  reaches out, only the silhouette
of a ghost flows through his fingers.
Perhaps the oblivious woman blinked.
Now vulnerable in public to women
shaped well, and frantic to disguise
his craving, now a crime, he pretends
  to see an old friend. He waves.

Museum Logic

Two gleaming brass figures
   —the man standing,
the woman's legs embracing
his waist, their twelve arms
gesturing wildly—play out
their self-absorbed drama
on top of another person.

      •

   Of course, beyond
the naive and desperate
hope of ethics, of politics,
   when distracted,
when dazed and dazzled,
we adore sex. And art,
I really meant to say art.
   Briefly, we resolve
   the essential vertigo
of our lives, then sleep.

      •

Please allow a sated person
   the darkness of sleep.
Please allow a dazed person
   the oblivious dream
of art. People subjected
to the fixed focus of light,
like tormented prisoners,
   can't relax or think.

      •

   Even a decent dogma
applied to a poem denies
the hidden functions of self,
   as when a propagandist,
designing banners, secretly
   uses his favorite colors.

Even people condemned
to live out the specific bias
of time and condition, of
money and pain, still honor
that monk who chants
all night in his cave.

Camera Obscura

A thinker lives his words
when typing no matter what
he thinks, as his fingers show.
If nothing else, his body,
    by adapting itself
to the shape of his chair,
limits the effect of his bias,
    though no one cares,
    or should care, unless
his words resemble a chair.

       •

The artist shaping a monument
to himself, a silhouette in space
that attracts birds and tourists,
a life formed in matter, can only
wave at criminals that run past.
We savor the monument's
consoling power while pain
continues to accrue in every
direction, but without effect,
    as though we only collect
those books we never open,
a kind of cemetery, you say.

       •

Since social forces obscure my sight
at a party I select a secluded spot,
like a spy, to stare at people
    moving their lips.
    In the distance the bomb
dropped from an invisible plane
    leaves behind an explosion
we can't hear: see that photo
    published after the war.

Why This Poem?

Its intentions are clear as the air in a beehive.
It's not a surrogate for a kind of absence.
 It declares itself like a finger. Cicero
would have kept this poem in a leather pouch
and carried it on his back as he fled the city.

Like Braille

The vast, shining variety
of simultaneous changes
complicates the uniform
atomism of time, just as bits
    of sand record without
distinction the temporary
shape of each foot. We trace
that thought in the shape
    of words, like a blind
person playing in sand.
              •

A noun uses a verb to locate
another noun to form a syntax
    that echoes life, whether
we like it or not, and thus
    presents that dimension
of time that can be thought
by a blind person at the beach.
    When, in tears, we peer
through that haze of regret,
of longing, our words change
    their syntax, their plot,
    to find a gin and tonic.
              •

The paper on which words
appear protects the reader
and writer from each other
while connecting their lives,
their meanings, and rearranging
    their money, that small sum.
After brushing aside each page
like a series of curtains, the reader
holds what's left of the writer
    in his hands, as when one
blind person embraces another.

The Largesse of Possibility

in words, those layers
of contradictory notation,
    establish the force
of a relativity so stringent
every proffered meaning
collapses. Like Europeans
who are depressed, and thus
    alert to displaced ideas,
the poet traces the entropic
    shifts of his own mind.
You only see an electron,
    he says, as a graph
of the emptiness in its wake.

•

Even a Balkan city under siege used
    a beauty contest to stimulate
    concern, while not far away
Muslim women were being raped.
The general noise of the world
    absorbed their screams.
    Selecting what we suffer,
when not involved, we reduce
    ethics to a fashion, a party,
an excuse to sample cheap wine.
Even Jesus postponed his prayer
    until that woman finished
washing his feet with her hair.
    More wine? he asked.

•

As thoughts overwhelmed
    by death must dissolve
    and disappear, as does
    that person who dies
    while thinking, those

thoughts exposed to life,
to the lurid grace of facts,
must expand, it seems,
    like an eager penis
when touched. Lovers
then absorb the sudden
shift of invisible electrons
    from one orbit
    to another.

After Halloween

Hasta la muerta todo es vida.
Cervantes, 1615

A true thought takes the time
    to think space into
the space of that thought
    moving through time,
the way the writer's sneeze
    interrupts his writing.
Since each logic contains a gap,
    I excuse my own lapses,
as any kind person would.

•

Still, it's true that what exists
    confirms, by the force
of its existence, the adroit
manner of its exposition,
as when a handless man
    waves goodbye.

•

A bullet flies through a brain
notably faster than the speed
of thought, and so solves
each problem it touches,
unlike the person shot.
The thinker only thinks
while still alive, strangely
    enough, as though
    the fact of life itself
shapes a thought. That
    person never sings
except inside his shower.

•

If no assertion survives
the implications of death,
     as one frantic German
sadly insisted, then really
each thought says nothing,
each word a mere ghost
     on Halloween.
     Neither the Buddhist,
engulfed by a vast light
     when he dies, nor
his friends, actually see
     that dead body glow.
                    •

In any sudden, cosmic flash
     of karmic revelation
     (the cartoon bulb
in each brain explodes)
     I'm stunned, too,
like a driver overcome
     by the glare of snow.
     Picture reincarnation:
that tired person at night,
     in his car, flashing
towards one blinding
     truck after another.

IV

PROPTER HOC

We assume that some movement
in the bodily organs is associated
sympathetically with all our thoughts.

Immanuel Kant, 1790

Tourist Attractions

A former girlfriend praises my new place
though wonders who the new ashtrays
    are for, so I mumble something
in one direction while glancing
the other way. In one mirror
    I catch her smiling to herself
in another mirror. What frantic lovers
    we were, especially on vacation
in Ireland, where our families began,
    where intense people evolve
    backwards in order to descend
from themselves. On a parchment map
    I brought back the rivers
of Ireland look like pieces of string.
From a satellite passing overhead
    we see the blanched ground
where nothing grew. The ancient path
    of English soldiers now shines
like a snail's trail in the moonlit night.
    A loose thread on her sweater
I remove while she searches the map
for some tiny trace of what happened.

Zeno's Paradox

Say you're haunted
by the woman you left
    but still loved and by
the woman who left you
still loving her, and by
words: the first woman
and then, later, the second,
when departing, took half
    your library, as part
of the informal settlement.
    While you lamented
anemic language, each
lugged cartons of books
    to her van. Thanks,
though, to Zeno's paradox,
no matter how often
    a woman takes half
your books, she'll never,
that way, get them all.
                    •

Actually, each time, almost
crying, you gave them up
gratefully, like a character
in a novel who admits regret,
    as though consigning
to the woman all those
    voices you heard
when not listening to her.
Now the volumes themselves
in your memory displace
    an awkward grief,
while the inaudible voices
    continue mumbling.

What's Repeated

Her best lover, a frail painter
whom you admire, because he smiles
sadly, attuned to pain or afraid
    he too might lose
her attention, asks in passing:
    "How you doing?"
    "Limping," you say.
    "I know what you mean,"
he says, "I *know* what you mean."
His repetition, like the refrain
in a great blues song, allows you
    at least to hear some echo
of her life—he's that generous.
             ●

Having sneaked in one morning
after being with him, she appears
    suddenly under the covers,
which she tosses aside, then leaves
you pressed like a fossil on the bed.
             ●

Even if she doesn't bathe for days
    her smell has the sweetness
of fermentation. Bruised apples
on the ground. Pictures are nice,
she says, but really only show
what's obvious, like a mirror.
The question finally you ask
    about him, she repeats,
playing for time, as though
what's repeated is the answer.

8888888888

That's it!
    Nietzsche, 1882

Only the generic, social engineer—
who ignores the mind's restrictions,
and each heart's helpless yearning,
and the naked body's naked demands,
    you know, those lewd details
on bathroom walls—still wonders why
    nothing really changes.

Talking only when questioned, unlike
pathetic people who spill their guts,
a reluctant Kelly finally told the poet
it was Tom she couldn't live without.
There's a kind of pain so intense
    it happens in slow motion.
    The poet pictured Kelly's legs
    (and the rapt focus of her will)
calmly adjusting to another person.
    That her anatomy only now
    appeared mysterious
suggested an odd, technical problem
for a dumb person dazed by sex.
    Since Tom was not just large
and smart, with muscles, but also
warmhearted, Kelly's attraction
seemed natural, like good weather.

                    •

    As though intrigued by failure,
Kelly enjoyed intellectuals. Her disdain
pleased her so much she remained
open to the very thing she doubted.
A clever lover's excessive language

stimulates flesh, which speaks,
in turn, like fingers typing words.

•

Once a cheerleader, kicking up
first one leg, then the other,
in her initial tribute to flesh,
Kelly Spires grinned to herself.
Dazed boys in a trance floated past
on the field. Already bohemian,
she mocked the silly sentiments
of pop music and smiling virgins
and people lying out in the sun.
Her own skin grew ever paler,
moist and powdery, like mushrooms
in a cave. Having read Kawabata
tales about fornication and tea
she collected Japanese prints.
Each small, leering man showed off
the colossal size of his penis.
Sometimes, she and her boyfriend,
at the porno drive-in, acted out
what they saw on the screen.

•

The poet pictured her reddish hair
over her face in the dark.
If he couldn't be the one whose feet
she anointed, he wanted somehow
to remain a part of the performance,
the dance. If not Jesus, then at least
John the Baptist, whose gaping head
got swirled about on a platter.
Thank you Salomé. Kelly told
erotic truths the way other women
try on socks. Sex happens. Big deal.
When a glacier moves, even smart
people scream. In her casual voice

her cosmic fables had the force
of science. He was happy then
just to work in her lab. If reminded
what her clothes barely contained,
her breasts a barometer of pressure,
she sympathized. "Men are such pigs,"
    she said, as she smiled.
This raunchy response, her comments
often a strip tease, kept him guessing.
Circe on her island also joked around.

•

Rather than a life, an intellectual
has thoughts. The poet recorded
abrupt sensations, like a seismograph,
    that shifting line on paper.
In and of itself, the "world worlds,"
    as a famous Nazi once claimed,
unlike Shakespeare, who exclaimed,
who pleaded: "World, world, O world."
That Kelly's mind, like her body,
    opened to any possibility
overwhelmed the attentive lover
    who noticed, and in that
was the magic of frantic sex.
The world rose again into view
like words from invisible ink.

•

Their gin glasses left moist circles
    among the cigarette burns
on the table. Seasoned by its scars,
    shiny in the semi-darkness,
like an antique mirror, the bar
    eased its patrons from care.
    The poet hoped to entertain
Kelly, to hold her attention,
but obliquely, like a cat in the dark.

About the origin of Kelly's reserve,
     her silence, in awe or dread,
or some crime, perhaps a vague abuse
or hormonal surge, perhaps a mind
     too finely tuned and accurate,
thus too precise to speak, the poet
had no idea, though certain, arcane
books, he'd heard, explain just that.

                    •

     In their booth by the window
     the half-drunk poet felt secure.
"How *did* you and I ever get started?"
     "You don't know?"
     "No," he said.
     "Really?"
     "Really."
"I put a spell on you," she said.
"What do you mean?"
     "Just that."
     "What kind of spell?"
"I'm not going to tell you," she said.
     Leaning over to caress his hand,
to reassure him, she showed instead
that her affection now was really
     just pity. Before, and before
     sex, she had wanted to be free,
it seemed, free of the responsibility
of choosing, and then, when freed,
still choose. "Of course," she said.

                    •

The poet's older women friends
thought Kelly's passive demeanor
     just another sly maneuver.
She had the haughty, lazy manner
of a renowned ballerina on vacation.
Men panted around her like dogs,

whose sniffing she accepted.
Pretty, but not a classical beauty,
she looked styleless, offhanded,
as though clothes only mattered
    on the floor. The conversion
of her disdain into the helpless
    frenzy of sex was thrilling.
The greedy compulsion of desire,
    her hunger, then softened,
as though freed from all the sad
    expectations of her life.

•

One night, when naked, the poet held
Kelly naked in his arms as she slept.
His skin, exposed to the pressure
of her body for hours, he hoped
    would retain that imprint
longer than a thought. Careful not
to wake her, reaching down, he parted
    her legs, which lazily adjusted
to his hand. His probing finger
    absorbed her mute response
    as she slept, her body swelling
into an unvoiced sigh, as the tremor
of those soft contractions, so endearing
    to him, then deepened her sleep.

•

At the bar, Kelly confessed
    finally that just drawing
figure-eights—8888888888,
    like a skater on ice
moving in a trance—was what
had put a spell on the poet.
This occultic conviction sounds silly,
of course. When a young woman,
who is wild and eager, is curious

57

to see a corpse at rest in its coffin,
    and a spindly hand reaches out
to touch her, please, don't blame
    the dead man, said the poet
to himself, as though convincing
    a skeptic. Swimming
    in her embrace, that man
    is helpless, like a salmon
            accepting fate.

                    •

"You mean you actually performed
a kind of ritual?" the poet asked.
"No," she said. "Not 'a kind.' Just
a simple, straightforward ritual."
The poet rattled the ice in his drink.
His drinking made his misery
more intense, more dramatic,
    like grand opera, and thus
important enough to endure.

                    •

Once, early on, when the poet asked
what she really expected for herself
    from Tom and him, considering
all their different needs, Kelly said:
"Everything!" as would the poet
himself, had he had her options.
Then she smiled, with inadvertent glee,
her sense of power. From the pleasure
of power, she saw in the poet's pain
    the confirmation of her power,
which then expanded even more.
    Neither angry nor resentful,
perhaps the poet was just older,
or just the happy victim of her skin,
    which glowed. Perhaps
    he loved her. He wanted

what he couldn't have, of course,
but never thought to demand it.
Desire, he thought, simply happens,
the way an embarrassed person
turns red. Even if his feeling
     for Kelly was inspired
        only by the mute underside
of great sex, just turning her over
on the bed, as still sometimes
she allowed, changed nothing.

●

Distracted, she watched the sullen,
unshaven, gorgeous bartender
mix drinks, as the poet watched her.
     Outside, the haze of dusk
had slowly deepened into darkness.
Lights in the bar brightened in response,
     like eyes suddenly opening.
Was that pale, sultry look, that glance
     of the vampire, was that what
made the bartender, and even a poet,
intriguing, as though all that Kelly
could see, all that anybody could see,
was just the halo effect of eyes?

●

A more careful person, of course,
might have calmed down enough
to think of other, fuller distinctions
before he lifted himself from the booth,
a bit heavy with drink, to find outside,
after kissing Kelly good-bye, his lips
holding hers a few, hungry seconds
     too long, that the world,
all around him, vaguely receded,
like the horizon, no matter where
     he actually decided to go.

Form and Content

The cautious writer who defers
judgment, feigning manners,
   who trusts only things
   he can't see, eventually
fashions from a blank hope
his own death. He holds
his breath forever behind
   the vacant contours
of his face, like a frightened
actor in a play. What happened
   was his lover had stopped
touching him without moving
her hand, so that she was there
but not there, was thinking
   of another person.

         •

Dedicated people who repress
introspection in order to change
the world, who affirm their own
death, and his, like Republicans
who stay married, he admires,
he resents. Only the obscenity
   of actual death nullifies
all distinctions, as when blood
   seeps from ruptured cells
after sex. But what happened
   was his lover had stopped
touching him without moving
her hand, so that she was there
but not there, was thinking
   of another person.
         •

The nervous guy glancing
always at the next woman

worships just that God
that disappears each time
a person prays. No wonder
his lover stopped touching
    him without moving
her hand, so that she was there
but not there, was thinking
    of another person.
                ●

The woman who refuses him,
    that thin dress concealing
    her secrets, keeps his ideas
    to herself. He understands
    nothing about compassion
    and tourists until her body
opens before him, like a book.
Of course, all the subconscious
    distortions implicit here,
he accepts, without knowing,
    of course, what they are.

V

AGE OF ENLIGHTENMENT

When you discourse with another, stand
not so near him as to breathe in his face.

Adam Petrie, 1720

Since the intimate focus of his lamp
      as he reads excludes the pain
and pathos of the world, the poet
      likes to live his life at night,
like a fugitive; he likes to hide,
      like a convalescent, inside
the permanent scenes of a book.

                    •

In class, the poet's opened book
reflects light on his face, like a halo,
      and he smiles, to confirm
with his students, who smile back,
the delicate possibility of meaning.
After class, the poet limps past
that fatuous dean who affirms
only the idea that fits his norm,
      the boxed space of a form,
      like a tall guy in a tiny bed
      at the dorm, who cries out.

                    •

Fusing together the two stereotypes
      they both admire, the florid
      Irish owner of the bookstore
offers the maudlin poet a glass
of whiskey, whose misty trance
is like a poem. Even their jokes
      invoke the archaic virtue
      and fluid grace of friends
from the literary world of drunks.
Sipping port while playing pool,
said David Hume, excites us
      more than thinking
      precisely about the sad limits
of thought. In the shared feeling
of relaxed ideas and schmoozing,
in the droll versions of a decent life,
each scene stands out, like a myth.